Pieces of Time

Thoughts of a Planner

by

Edward Grant-Gila Pulagis

Nenge Books

Pieces of Time - Thoughts of a Planner
by Edward Grant-Gila Pulagis

Copyright text and photos © Edward Grant-Gila Pulagis 2021.
Picture page 6: Copyright © Sean Ova 2021 used by permission.

All rights reserved.

Without limiting rights under the copyright above, no part of this publication shall be reproduced, stored in or introduced into a retrieval system in any form or by any means (electronic, mechanical, photocopy, recording or otherwise) without the prior written permission of the publisher of this book.

Design and desktop by Nenge Books
Published by Nenge Books, Australia, August 2021
ABN 26809396184
nengebooks1@gmail.com
www.nengebooks.com

Nenge Books publishes quality books using print-on-demand technology to provide cost effective results for small and large print runs for independent authors. Author enquiries are welcome to nengebooks1@gmail.com

ISBN 978-0-6488206-9-7

Dedication

Dedicated to my brother Albert T Pulagis.
For the 25 years of your life I took this inspiration to write out my thoughts.
Heaven gained a beautiful soul.

THERE COMES A TIME WHEN YOU WILL REALIZE THAT THE PEOPLE WHO CARE ABOUT YOU MOST ARE THE ONES THAT YOU SPEND LESS TIME WITH.

Grant-Gila

Contents

One Journey - Psalms 91	7
The Pieces of Time	9
For your greatness lies in humility	11
A Saviour I Need Everyday	12
At Your Feet	13
O My Wretched Heart	15
Take over from this broken road I am taking	17
My Deliverer and My Strong Tower!	18
My Eyes	20
God I am down and hurt	22
Four Men	24
Face to Face with My Maker	26
In the Midst of their Struggle	27
Against the Wind I Thrived	29
And Soared Higher I Flew	31
Through the Wind I Drew Strength	32
One Day	34
An Angel that Went to Heaven	36
In the silhouette of a female, I see the real woman	38
A love that never fails	39
God calls me by my name	40
The Fisher of Man	42
Somebody, Nobody - Mr Body	44
There is a Rugby Pitch	46
To the well-known	47
Dreams of a Nation	48
O Lord, One Last Shot	50
The Rose in God's Garden	51
Beneath the Rainbow Sky	53
Dreams of a Dreamer	54
0.099%	55
He walks on this road	57
Outside of the Box	58
Bridge	60
Thirty-five minutes	63
The Gift	65
This Christmas	66
A Moment in Time	68
The Thorn of Roses	69
Even King Solomon's Words of Love	70
Kindness in Words	71
Your character and wit I cannot comprehend	73
I'm a Fighter	74
If you were	76

One Journey – Psalms 91

Papua New Guinea land of a thousand images
Song of the bird of paradise sung in 800 plus different languages
A people born in a nation of many cultures
Land of a million adventures
Mountains filled with hidden treasures
Seas filled with beautiful islands beyond the shores

9 million people, one country
1 nation, one journey.

The Pieces of Time

The pieces of Time
Pitted on top of the highest climb
Contained in a jar of dime
Written in the writers prime

The pieces of memories
Written in the writer's stories
Carved out of the mountain of quarries
Imprinted on the parchment of life histories

The pieces of time hold unforgettable sadness
Events that took away a child's happiness
Broken years of a teenager's gladness
Lived out on the streets of Quail Cres

Days are fresh in the writer's tears
Months that filled with challenging fears
All overcome through the writer's years
As a life is shaped through many prayers

The hardships of a young teenager,
Begins the incredible journey of a foreigner
The Author's pen is raising up a deliverer
For the journey is so much greater

Whose journey shall traverse into distant places
Walking into cities of many faces
Encountering countries of many races
People whose lives changed his paces

From all the hardships,
Came the many good friendships
To building blocks of memorable mateships
Where bread and wine were broken in fellowships

The Grand Weaver opening all doors of success
Each eloquently shaped in many process
Written in the writers' achievements
Confirming God's fulfilments

The pieces of time unfolding the blessings
In the writer's life settings
The pieces of time held firmly in God's hand
Written in the life of the writers stand

The pieces of time
Written in the writer's planning career
The pieces of time
Working in a cross culture breaking a barrier

A planner of cities
Travelling across nations of many entities
The pieces of time
Written in the writer's prime.

For your greatness lies in humility

Father pick me up from this broken road,
I want to follow in your footsteps,
Beside the great stream of waters,
For your greatness lies in humility

Father in my integrity, I walked in unrighteousness
In great steps my path saw blindness
With extinguishable strength you carry me
For your greatness lies in humility

In fleeting moments, I encountered darkness
In terrible mistakes, I saw difficulties
My soul bearing the scars of time
There my pride led me to great humility

In a world of unknown path
Lord I pursue after your truth
Bounded in your love and tranquillity
For your greatness lies in humility

A Saviour I Need Everyday

A Saviour I need everyday
On my knees I pray
I cry out to you forsake me not!
In the shadow of darkness so low
My beseeching heart is yours for warmth,

A feel of strength
A touch of comfort
I would rather walk with you in the night
Then to walk alone in the light
A Saviour I need everyday

At Your Feet

I sleep tonight,
A lonely knight,
At your feet in delight

At your feet I am safe and secure
All the challenges I can endure
In your unbounded love so pure

The world searches for me
So, I will run first to be at your feet
Where my future is guaranteed

At your feet I worship you
You are worthy of praise
My entire hope is in you

O My Wretched Heart

O my wretched my heart
Full of the scars of sin
O my wretched soul
Full of unrighteousness

My thoughts wonder off
When my heart is set on high things
What can cleanse my thoughts?
Only the blood of Jesus can make me whole

The condition of my heart is delicate
It cannot guard my thoughts
Where my mind slips into the hallways of pleasure
God rescues me from it with his love

Jesus, to think I am better than you
I am ashamed and so I worship you!
my hope is in yours, my heart's desire
Is to know you more

As my soul delights
That I am truly yours
My soul rejoices in such joy
In fulfilment to all of life's challenges

Take over from this broken road I am taking

Take over from this broken road I'm taking
Like a broken ship my faith is sinking
Fill my cup for I thirst after thee
My utmost desire is to follow your lead

In sin I try to hide but great is your mercy indeed
It brought me out and freed me from bitter resentment
This is how much your love is my total fulfilment
Your face I continuously seek in encouragement

My heart repents from unforgiveness
Now teach me true loving kindness
As I learn obedience like the graceful dove
My vision is now focused above

Teach me a rock like faith
To be courageous in the shadow of death
To be steadfast in your word of encouragement
To be my staff of strength!

My Deliverer and My Strong Tower!

O sacred love my flower
Listen to the words of your lover
This is a tribute to God my strong tower!

My deliverer and my strong tower!
My love, my beautiful flower
This God is my deliverer,

In sickness He is my healer,
In brokenness He is my restorer,
In distress He is my rescuer,

The ultimate conqueror of all conqueror
The redeemer of all Redeemer
He is the Son of the Most High

Mountains of PNG behold my King!
Upon him I will conquer over you that very thing!
I will shift the seven mountains of the world

Each mountain is within the reach of the Father
They are the hidden treasures of darkness
The Christ in me is the pinnacle to my success

O sacred love my flower
Listen to the words of your lover
This is a tribute to God my strong tower!

My Eyes

My eyes are beautiful
But they are filled with tears of sorrow
I do not worry about tomorrow
It is my brother, the longingness to see him

To hug him in my arms forever in heaven
And enjoy one day with the saints
God you've walked alone on this road before
On all of earths shattered road

My eyes are fearfully and wonderfully created
To see the world around me
Today this day I see clouds of grey
My feet treading gently on a rainy day

My eyes are a strategic piece of my entire being
They are the gateway to life's coming attractions
Therefore, they must first focus on the Christ within!
His hands constantly guide my path

My eyes discern the direction of where my mind is looking
As I plan for the future things to come
I make room for changes to happen
All things for the good of those who love God

My eyes test my attitude
They test my character and all that is in me
They see how I react to all of life's coming attractions
They test the waters of my emotions under extreme conditions

My eyes have seen all the seasons of life
In the days of war and peace I have seen
There were times of plenty and much joy
Through moments of death and sadness

My eyes have seen the miraculous wonder working power of Jesus
He changed my life on a day nobody thought possible
When the world walked out, I received my calling upon my life
He walked into my life, I was chosen at this very moment

God I am down and hurt

God I am down and hurt
My nights are getting bleak,
My strength getting weak

I cannot see another day
Bad as it is was today
Then it was everyday

My wounded heart no one cares
No one but you who shares
Crying silently, I'm on my knees

Though I am at ease
A day without you I cannot see
On the path I am going through

Where my life is like a flowing stream
O Lord that is so true!
For my emotions rest on your lovely beam

Refresh my soul a broken plater
For there is none that most matter
O God why have you left me in my plight?

In a place of light!
For you found me in a place of night
In the night I held onto your hands

As darkness swarmed all around us
I questioned how long will I feel this way
God I am down and hurt

I am once again on the cliff's edge
I want to give up this life suppressed in a wedge
I am losing focus for my life is over the hedge

Four Men

Four men in separable to each other,
Despite differences are four,
Remained united in heart forever more,

Four men with a special love for each other,
Men under the test of times still remain strong,
Men of all seasons with character as solid as rock,

Four men supported each other through life,
Ordinary men raised under difficult situations,
Put through life's extreme conditions,

Four regions gave birth to Papua New Guinea
Not the perfect family but a good country
Four brothers raised by a British Father

Four sisters raised by an Australian Mother
A mother's touch of love like a stroke of feather
Not the perfect mother but a loving one

Brothers are they, the Papuan,
Family in diversity are they, the Momasean,
Unity through many are they, the Highlander,
Land of abundance are they, the New Guinea Islander,

Born in 1975 are these four men,
Four generations onwards,
Many sons & daughters they have raised!

Through the highs and lows they thrived to survive,
40 years on the four men continue to stand firm,
This is an example to unite us all!

Face to Face with My Maker

Face to face with my maker
In awe one sweet day
Face to face with my maker
Oh, how glorious that day

Face to face with reality
Transformation in life eternity
That one day I will be at home
In the city more beautiful than Rome

For I am heaven bound
A sheep that was found
Face to face with my maker
Jesus, you created me a leader

I am your follower
You are my healer
On that cross I now put all my trust
Giving all my life with a strong thrust

You looked at me with love
Over my sinful life and like a dove
You brought me Salvation
A moment of repentance led to pure fascination

A Saviour is the one I shall see
When the time comes, I shall sail beyond earths sea
Into the sunset of heaven where I shall see my maker
There I shall stand face to face with my Creator

In the Midst of their Struggle

In the midst of their struggle
Are men of courage
Their story is born,
Acts of courage and resilience,

From one generation to the next,
Their story is to be told,
How they lived, walked, talked,
For the legacy continues on

Men of courage walking through the night
Into the morning light of a bright future
Light of hope sets at the end of the tunnel
a hope of unlimited blessings

Rare with values exceeding the jewels of a princess,
Hidden within them are identities of success,
World Leaders and Giant killers entrapped in them,
Ready to be unleashed as blue prints of achievements,

Their purpose cannot be torn,
A covenant is established between each and their maker,
Their purpose of existence is in their Creator,
Who is also their source and founder,

You men of courage rise up!
This is your time to speak,
The world needs men to take their place,
Face the challenges of today as an overcomer

Be empowered by the Word of God
Death, you tried separating them
But they separated you
You tried but you couldn't

Scattered beyond the ends of the earth
The destiny of Papua New Guinea lies in you
Men of courage be bold as lion!
Women of faith be vigilant as the eagle!

Against the Wind I Thrived

Against the wind I thrived,
Against the wind I wavered,
Against the wind I faltered,
Against the wind my course was altered

Like the sailor lost at sea I swam,
Through seas of time my life was caught in a dam,
Like the storm I went through hardships so treacherous,
This is my life journey on earth beautifully dangerous

Beyond New Ireland's beautiful swaying palm
My lifepath took me into the night of experience so calm,
So begun my path, I walked beyond Lae's fertile valleys
Light of God shown over my journey through a thousand miles

Against the wind I struggled,
to fly my destiny through cloudy hays
Against the wind my dreams I protected
Under the humid conditions of Port Moresby days

Against the wind my challenges I fought
Against the wind solutions I thought
Against the wind the sacrifices of my brother
Gave me enough strength to walk into my future

To gain a far brighter future filled with hope
I had to go down many mistakes like a hilly slope
Challenges were like the force of wind, but I ran,
against the wind and I had great fun

Against the wind when things looked bad, I still smiled
Against the wind when situations arise, I still laughed
Against the wind I had moments where I cried
For the test in my life were real, I faced

Against the wind of change I overcome
I understood that a statesman I shall become
Against the wind I learned that I can still fly
Amidst the problems I soared higher above the sky

Against the wind I survived the skies
I attained more knowledge in the wilderness
I received more understanding in the seas
All these I am learning to be patient and at ease.

And Soared Higher I Flew

And soared higher I flew
Darkness and light become one to me,
the heavens above, the world beneath me
against the wind I survived under the grace of God
against the wind I rose to success
against the wind I flew above the storm
against the wind I was tamed
what anyone thought I could not do, I flew beyond
And soared higher I flew.

Through the Wind I Drew Strength

Through the wind I drew strength
I drew closer to Him over times length
I discovered that there is more than this life
Beyond my challenges and my strife

My knowledge attained more understanding,
And they thought me wisdom of right standing
Like an eagle these prepared me to glide the winds
And grace my destiny to run swiftly on deer's hinds,

To the way of the King's
I accumulate treasures the world brings,
My steps God guided into the high places
Known as the heights of the skies

Sky's that showed the secrets of the wind
Against the might of the earth
And the hardness of the dearth
I flew much stronger

Like the courageous eagle
My attitude is firm as the eagle's beak
Like the eagle I knew my strengths
And I knew my weakness

Eliminating the sky's vultures,
The secular cultures,
Through challenges the man becomes complete
Against the world's best to compete

For He is Heaven's finest,
Indeed, to become good you have to be the best
To reach the pinnacle one must passed the test
To be successful in life you must serve without protest

One Day

One day a father sent out a boy
To find his toy
Away from his comfort zone
A young man all alone
He walked until he was out of his zone
His path led into a distant city,
He found nothing pretty
But the capital city
An awful sight what a pity
In all this God was good
He provided shelter, clothing and gave him food
He brought back a complete man
Who now stands before a Congress of men
To show his father
A complete man
To surprise an angel mother
A Prime Minister in the beginning
As it was spoken in the right timing
All in the storm
A boy is shaped into form
Drawing out the man in a boy
Not a created toy
All in a male
Not in a female
All in a man
Not in a woman
Who now stands a real man
A God made millionaire
Not a biological Billionaire.

An Angel that Went to Heaven

An angel that went to heaven so young
A life so beautiful
An angel that went to heaven
Who lived a simple life
Amidst his struggles and strife

He was never famous
Never glamorous
Left a void in my family
A life filled with dreams
An angel now in heaven

Gone with the wind
An angel that went to Heaven
Left our hearts broken
It continuous to bleed with pain
An angel that went to heaven

Left me sad and alone
An angel that is now in heaven
My best man on that special day
But there won't be a memory as such on this day
For he is now in heaven

An angel in heaven
Guarding me each day as I walk on earth
Alone in the night I walk the streets of Waigani
Watching me with your smile
Hugging me when I cry

Because I miss him everyday
And when I go to work with sadness in my heart
He encourages me not to give up on my dreams when I feel like it
Because he sees my destiny that one day, I will become a great man
With a bright and great future

I thank you Lord
For this brother of mine
An angel that went to heaven
for these 24 years I've been so blessed
I will see him one day

In the silhouette of a female, I see the real woman

In the silhouette of a female, I see the real woman
In the figure of a male, I see the man
There were many males but very few man
In the woman, I see the beauty of her heart

In the image of the man God drew out the real man
And taught me the pain of sweet success
He gave me more joy and unlimited blessings!
In the silhouette of a woman, I met my wife from Sariba

Her skin white and fine as the sands of Samarai
Her face pretty and clear as the waters of Milne Bay
Her hair long, curly and straight,
Jet black and soft as fine sago

Knowing her life is discovering her dreams
my visions integrate with her plans
Amidst the strife are my plans as our bodies become one soul
In his garden God woke me up from the sleep

Years of working and tendering God's Garden
Have led me to this moment
A moment He warned not to slip
Like an eagle I am designed to fly above the storm

This is a unique story of two dreamers
At the highest point in the sky, I met my own kind
In the silhouette of the woman, I see her character
A very rare find is Mulaweta

A love that never fails

A love that never fails
A love that never fails, a love that never boasts
A love not jealous, a love less of pride
A love of patience and humility

A love forever
A love forever faithful
A love forever faithful and courageous
A love forever faithful, courageous and hopeful

A love so true
A love so true, uniting two hearts,
Uniting two hearts, living in one body
Living in one body, conditioned to endure the different seasons

Enduring different seasons is a love that is kind and gentle
A love that is kind is like a gentleman
Like a gentleman, he is not self-seeking
He is not self-seeking or easily angered

Because he is not easily angered, he doesn't force his will upon her
And keeps no record of wrongs
He forgives and moves forward
- the one true love who will never leave you

God calls me by my name

Satan knows my name
But he calls me by my sin
because he hates me
God knows my sin
but he calls me by my name
because he loves me

God knows my mistakes
but he calls me by my name
because he sees my potentials
he knows my credentials
God knows my sin
but he calls me by my name
because he forgives

God calls me by my name
he sees my struggles
and he knows how much I have tried
he knows my every thought
he sees the tears that fall
and he hears me when I call
he tells me he has a great plan for me
for he is my father
and he sees the blood of Jesus in me

God calls me by my name
he sees the wounds I carry
and the pain inside
he carry's my burdens

God calls me by my name
he knows my future
that has an expected end
a plan of hope with success
God knows my weakness
he calls me by my name
because he knows I am strong

God knows the lowest point of my life
for he has been there
he knows there is a point of elevation
God knows how much I have failed
still, he calls my name
because he knows I am a fighter
and I will never give up
he gives me answers to be determined
God knows how many times I fall
but he encourages me to get up
because he knows he will pick me up
God simply calls me by my name

The Fisher of Man

Out in the sea is the fisher of man,
with his jerrycan
Serving the Master,
from Munster

He walked the seashore
Surveys the sea ferries on the foreshore
Serving the Master each day
from the coast to the bay

The blue marlin one of his prized catch
On the boat is his net a firm patch
On the rod is his fishing line
The yellow fin rare and fine

The fisherman everyday he hooks, baits and throws,
The fishing lines among the meadows,
Every day he tries not to forfeit,
The work or slumber in defeat

Long hours of work have shaped his muscle
It is his duty, so it is not a tussle
His passion burns fiercely like a flame
But still humble without fame

His eyes are like a pure celestial fire more than
the light of the sun breaking through the den
his energy to work burns
To each success he makes huge returns

The fisher of man
Once a farmer back then
But that changed during the fall
Now a fisherman he is complete in all

Out in the sea he follows
Into the dark shallows
He baits the hook and the net he cast,
for there are souls that need saving fast

The fisherman stands complete in all
On the Nw Ireland shore
A fisherman who stands tall
One like never before

Somebody, Nobody - Mr Body

Not far away from the Parliament lives the hard-working Nobody
In the Government is the Member of Parliament Mr Somebody
Though Mr Nobody earns enough for today
It's nowhere near to what the politician earns everyday
In a world of politics where rules can bend
All these scrupulous activities have an end

And where sinners live righteously
While honesty is viewed a crime, seriously?
What about the Judiciary of demagogues?
In a court of dialogues,
Written in endless monologues,
The PNG bureaucracy is it still the milking cow?

A treasury belonging to Jack Wanpis
Just like the famous story
Jack had a cow named Public Finance raised in Waigani
Who once lived in a farmhouse named DSIP built into two storey

Along came uncle Joe Blow who used to hunt magani
Stole poor Jack's cow
While somebody's crying
Nobody's trying

And Mr Body's running
Away he goes hiding
Like a child, are you kidding?
That's a full-grown homo Sapien!

In Parliament,
Not far away from the Streets,
lives Somebody
Riding the Government

There is a Rugby Pitch

In a higher place
How so?
So, you think?
I guess they play rugby in heaven
That's what I think
Just like Evan Craven
Who used to play cricket,
Because of the ticket
He switched code to rugby union at jersey seven
Rugby in heaven a gentleman's game
What a way to put a name
Is it funny for he must be playing rugby
That grubby
Lovely, ruddy sport
He had a special place in that flanker spot

To the well-known

To the well known
I must now glide into the unknown
To capture my vision
And my mission
Beyond where she is
Sojourn in distant places
Together with many faces
Setting forth the coming of a generation against the wind,
Flying through the wind finding my purpose
Beyond the wind to finally see my future
Without the wind I can never be who I am
Do not fear my soul you must face the wind of your life!
For only against the wind, you will find your true self
I must ride the winds of the earth,
and face it
Close up to it and race it
Only against the wind the eagle learns to fly well
In many efforts to try
my wings I began to learn
with the wind beneath my wings
I will fly gracefully
I will fly beautifully

Dreams of a Nation

Dear Father, today was a pretty tough day
I've got many challenges, but I do not worry
For I know you will take care of me

Well, I guess you heard, I've been dreaming lately
I have big plans to become a good planner of the country someday
To serve my country well at the highest level one day

But I still wonder if you still dream about me
I dream about my people
I dream when I see young men & women on the streets

I dream when I see the injustice done to my people
Corruption is eating the moral fabrics of PNG
I am determined to slay and kill the famous giants of my time

When I see nation rise against nation
I dream about my country
I dream about the world & its people

I pray somewhere in between we will seek you
when nobody wants to make a stand
And make a difference for a child

To bring back hope for a brother, a father, a mother, a sister,
To bring justice to a widow, a family, a community,
To build a future for a people, a province and a country,

I dream to stand for the difference and truth
If you did not choose me, I would have not chosen you
I am truly privileged to call you my father

I dream how to improve the public service & the government
I dream about hospitals, science, roads, agriculture, business
I dream about development planning and technological breakthroughs,

I dream about peace, justice, law and order
Schools, well planned towns and cities

I have a vision for wealth and prosperity
Well Father I just simply have too many dreams
But this one I long for,

I dream to govern my nation with your wisdom,
To seek greater knowledge & understanding
That whatever plans I have in my heart I want you to have it all

Make it better for me
For I know you dream about me
It is the best dream ever from a loving Father!

O Lord, One Last Shot

To my goal one last shot
I am humbled for this opportunity on the dot
I am thrilled one last hope
I am thankful one more day
I am ever grateful one more beauty
That smile in the shadow of doubt I see
Ever more my faith is in Christ
Then on fire and suddenly grow cold
Nights that are bleak and wet with tears
In the morning sun shines
The warmth of joy calms the sea in me
One last shot O God
Though the pace seems slow
I will succeed with another blow
Success is failure turned inside out
To many more attempts one last shot
Is never the end
Because I am a fighter, I never give up
They are all I got to unwrap my blessings my dreams
An eternal investment of my future
Within me and their generations after.

The Rose in God's Garden

There are many roses
But I desire the rose in God's Garden
The rose planted in heavenly soil
She is very beautiful
The rose is God's heartbeat
She is God's creation and masterpiece
The white crimson of the West
And the red fragrance of the East
Put together is God's finest
Who created her?

Why the gardener whose garden Adam tendered and took care of
He is the one of course!
Displaying the mind of the great Creator
Adam desired for that rose
God put him to sleep and brought his desire out of his mind
And presented him this rose

I desire to be with God's rose in his beautiful garden
With fresh green grass
Trees of all kinds so colourful,
Flowers filled with pleasant fragrance
Planted on a land laid out perfectly
Filled with mansions of unique architectural design
That would take your breath away
For you can only find them in his garden
But above all there stands the rose

I sometimes wonder why my eyes fell for God's rose and not any other

I also wonder why I'm genuinely interested in that rose in my visions

I often ask who put that rose in my mind?

Then I remember Adam's tale it was my desire that open the eyes of my heart

My heart before time is attracted and shaped to fit her rosy soul

It dawns to me God specifically planted and nurtured that rose for me

So that one day I will pick it out from his garden

How can I love you my God when you know my love is not always perfect?

Teach me now to love ad cherish you and your rose forever

With honour, love and respect

For I dreamed one day I will marry my rose from the West

The rose in God's Garden.

Beneath the Rainbow Sky

Beneath the rainbow sky she danced
Beneath the rainbow sky he chanced
Beneath the rainbow sky she smiles
Beneath the rainbow sky he counts the miles
running along the river of Niles
Beneath the rainbow sky they meet
Faith in the bond of two hearts between
Beneath the rainbow sky she cries
Beneath the rainbow sky he tries
The highs and lows of two hearts in one body
Beneath the rainbow sky is just the two of them and nobody
Standing by the sea watching a beautiful sunset going down
Near a road built beside a beautiful town
Beneath the rainbow night she lays her head on his shoulder
Beholding the beauty of her eyes in the Creator
Her hair jet black and down to her waist,
Kissing her lips a sweet taste
The touch of her skin white and smooth,
On her image of beauty under the moon
Looking up into the wonder of the stars in the night
Shining colours of love through sky light
Beyond the celestial beings is God the holder
He is the perfect storyteller.

Dreams of a Dreamer

O grand weaver
Would I know her as my wife?
That Milne Bay from your beautiful garden
And get to know an imperfect person perfectly
Will I one day take her out on our first date?
Will I get to propose to her someday?
Would I ever marry that Milne Bay girl?
I can only imagine her in my arms
To share the moments of joy and happiness
Pain and hardships
To hug her when she is sad
And be the pillar of hope and foundation for our family

Should I stop talking about her?
O grand weaver if only I could quieten those questions
And listen to your words
Because you know my thoughts better
My heart beats faster every time I think of you
Because the grand weaver is also the Master planner
Now I know that behind my life there is a father
He is the designer of my destiny
He brings these converging strands of her life and my life
Into a composite whole so that two people one
They become the grand instrument,
through whom he uses for his purposes
Now I know that I am not dreaming,
you are the dreamer
I am your dream
We are your plan.

0.099%

She once told me of my chances
Of going out with her is slim
I had limited opportunities for my dances
In the evening, the lights became dim

She once told me not to get my hopes high
But the friendship still thrived
Amidst the low points I knew I'd survived
Like the underdog my breakthrough drew nigh

At 0.099% it looks impossible, but I'll make it
Though it tarries at 0.099% I'll take it
At 0.099% our friendship is at stake, but I'll protect it
At 0.099% my aim is her heart, so I'll shape it.

He walks on this road

Keeping his vision straight for the road is long
Shifting his gaze on the everglades beyond this road
Surveying the skies of a coming storm
With long strides of calm and courage he girts his belt
Tightens his grip on his bag slung over his shoulder
Heads bent and eyes forward he runs his hands over his scruffy beard
Alone on this fine weather
The eagles keeping him company in the day
The stars guide him through the night
Plotting out his destiny drawn into the memory of his mind
Sketch into the heart of his soul
Printed well into the image of his body
His boots slick and shiny flickers the sun's rays
His head covered with a cowboy hat, shot like a westerner
A John Wayne or Pierce Brosnan he looks like an outlaw
But this isn't a movie script, this is real!
This is a pilgrim walking on this road alone.

Outside of the Box

Every thread in our lives matters
Had I been selected I wouldn't have met you
Outside of the box I am

Inside of the box you are
The intellect from Divine Word
The Master's graduate from Flinders

Every thread matters
Because there is a Grand Weaver
His name is God

Outside of the box I am
The man with the streety Lae accent
But every thread matters

Because your path crossed mine
under Australia Awards
The prestigious scholarship

I met my match
I took the challenge
Every thread matters.

Copyright © Edward Grant-Gila Pulagis 2021

Bridge

In Australia there is a bridge
Standing between Adelaide & Sydney
a bridge of friendship between Dibinai
and Namatanai
Designed to close the ridge

From the distance the bridge lies straight
It stretches from the Torres Strait
Over the vastness of the Simpsons Desert
It connects two destinations, in two people, in one heart

WhatsApp, bridges the gap to the future
Phone creates the structure
Texting lays out the planning
The poems do the painting
And God completes the bridge designing

Thirty-five minutes

Thirty-five minutes
We sat together at the departure
Drinking chocolate and mocha

Just like the State of Origin Game
Or the restaurant we ate together
Or the day trip to circular Quay

Thirty-five minutes
Amongst anticipating passengers
Airport full of people

Memories of our first meet
At Sydney airport
A boy meets a girl

Thirty-five minutes
Been waiting to tell her in person
"I like you; I love you…"

A moment of silence
No reply, no response
Just casual "goodbyes"

Thirty-five minutes
Is a moment worth more than,
Those texting and hours of chatting

All of these
Are priceless moments
Written in the sands of time

But none of these
Were quite as fine,
As thirty-five minutes spent with you

It might sound silly
When I say
I treasure the thirty-five minutes

Please don't think that
The other times
Are not memorable

It's just that all these meets
Spanning all these days
Over the six months

Is a moment in time
The best thing ever
Is meeting you again for 35 minutes

The Gift

The best thing I ever received
Was given some time ago
So precious and rare
More valuable than gold

My heart beat faster
And my pulse began to race
I'll never forget that moment
Including time and place

We don't always agree on things
Sometimes we even fight
Anytime I return under your wings
We always set things right

So, the best gift ever
infiltrated my heart
I plan to keep you always
Forever to start

This Christmas

This Christmas close by the fire I sit
To warm my chilling feet a bit
Or with Rudolph the red nose reindeer, explore
All the snow-capped mountains I've seen before

From the first moment I saw you
The emotions were there
Hanging from my shirt sleeves
With tender loving care

Milne Bay, she sits on the white sandy beaches of Samarai
New Ireland, he stands to the cool breeze of Namatanai,
She watches the sunset go down in Alotau
He watches the moon go up from Kavieng, though,

every experience with you,
Makes my heart pitter patter
The gifts and the food
None compares to the matter

As my heart keeps beating
Strong and sure
Pumping loudly
For the one I adore

As we embark on the holiday
Enjoying each day
Treasuring this time
My heart grows fuller
As I know you are mine.

A Moment in Time

A State of Origin Game
A restaurant we ate together
A day trip to Manly Beach

A first meet at the airport
A city Sydney
A boy meets a girl
A priceless moment

All of these
Were quite as fine
As the day's I've spent with you

It might sound silly
When I say
I love those days a bunch

Please don't think that
The other times
Are not enjoyable, Erica

It's just that all these meets
Spanning all three days
Over the first few months

Are a moment in time
The best thing ever
Was meeting you

The Thorn of Roses

The thorn of roses
In order for the rose to bloom well
It must have thorns to protect it to tell,
Of its beauty developed through seasons never closes

Red as wine and white as snow
Bright as the suns light beyond the bow
Someday it will become beautiful as the roses on your profile picture
A scent of a sweet honey
A colour of a thousand feature
A value cannot be bought by money

Even the brave has fears
Even the warrior cries painful tears
Even the courageous have weaknesses
Boldness, in utter determination they face challenges

Don't break the friendship
even when the sun closes,
and the waves break on the horizons bliss
The friendship of roses

Even King Solomon's Words of Love

If I had the words to describe my feelings for you,
I would be the happiest man in the universe.
But let my words be few,
Because words seem to fail me time and time again,

Even King Solomon's words of love
Is not enough to express how I feel about you
Like the island in the storm peeking in the night
My love for you is genuinely fierce like the flames of fire

It burns away all of my heart's desire
It shapes and test my heart
Like the oceans tide it overflows in patience
Through the test of time my love for you is steadfast

Kindness in Words

Kindness in words creates confidence
Kindness in thought creates understanding
Kindness in giving creates love

Kindness in love creates patience
Kindness in patience creates peace
Kindness in peace creates goodness

Kindness in goodness creates gentleness
Kindness in obedience creates joy
Kindness in faithfulness creates discipline

Your character and wit I cannot comprehend

Nor will I fully understand your emotions to apprehend
But this I know she is the daughter of the eastern star of PNG
Where the sun rises over her, she is very beautiful
A province next to the nation's LNG plant

My thoughts of you are pure
Just like the sea meeting the beach I see my future
I look at you and I see proverbs 31, she is rare
I never made a mistake when I first pursued my friendship with you
At the very end of the street where two strangers met at the seventh avenue

It was like a movie scene when a boy meets a girl
At the corner of café 'curl'
It was like a dream
Except it is real for they were in the same team!

This happened under the sun
When a woman walks out of the sunset of friendship
To a man, a mother's son
So those two hearts will become one in a relationship.

I'm a Fighter

I'm a fighter
And I'm going train hard to be better
I'm a fighter
Therefore, I'm still in the fight for my flower

I'm a fighter
And I'm going to marry her someday
On a beach wedding somewhere one day
Her dreams I keep as the ultimate protector

My love is fierce over Sariba
The Warrior from Samarai
She is my cohort
I am her "buddy" from Namatanai
And she is beautifully hot

I'm a fighter
Born and raised in Lae
Trained in POM ready to play
A man made of clay

She is a fighter
Born and raised in Alotau
Went to Unitech Lae, even though,
She completed her studies years ago

She is a fighter
for the scholarship she was discouraged
But took courage
And graduated with a higher knowledge

I will marry her someday
Somewhere, pretty soon one day
In a lifetime I know this dream is real for that day
On the shores of Milne Bay

If you were

If you were an apple fruit, I'll pick you
If you were a flower, I'll protect you
If you were a friend, I'll stand by you

If you ever get tired, if you ever feel like giving up
I'll be your arms to carry your dreams and run with it!
I'll be that quite still voice saying "keep on, I am with you. You got this!"

If you were an angel, I'll be your wings, so that you can fly your visions
If you were a bee, I'll be the nectar, together we will produce the best honey
If you were the sand, I'll be the river to keep you cool

If you were the sun, I'll be the cloud to give you shade
If you were the eagle, I'll be the storm to give you strength to fly higher
If you were the swan, I'll be the lake for you to swim in

If you were a star, I'll be the night so that you can shine bright like a diamond for the world to see,
If you were a mountain climber, I'll be the mountain for you to stand on,
If you were here right now, I'll just simply smile and put my arms around you.

www.ingramcontent.com/pod-product-compliance
Lightning Source LLC
Chambersburg PA
CBHW051540010526
44107CB00064B/2793